I0817488

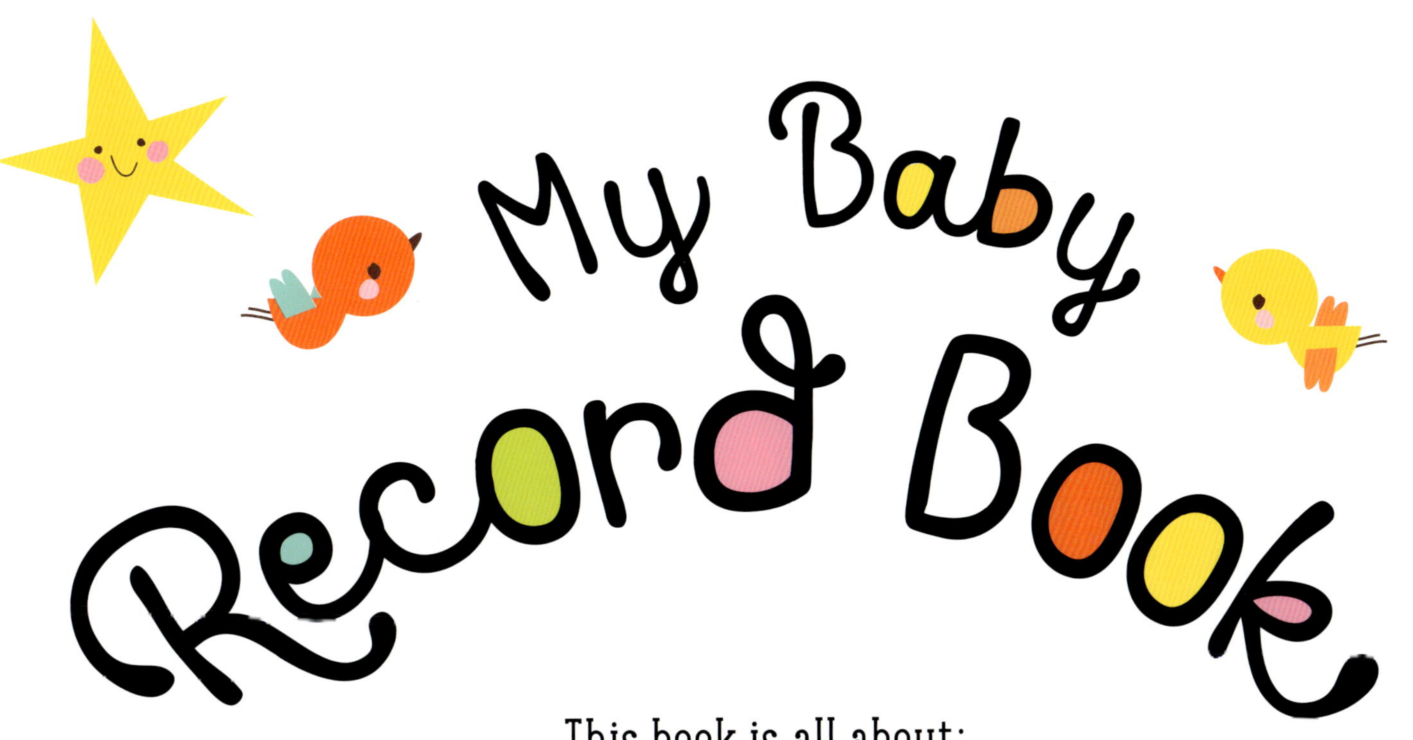

This book is all about:

....

photo

make believe ideas

My Family Tree
photo of my father
photo of me
photo of my mother

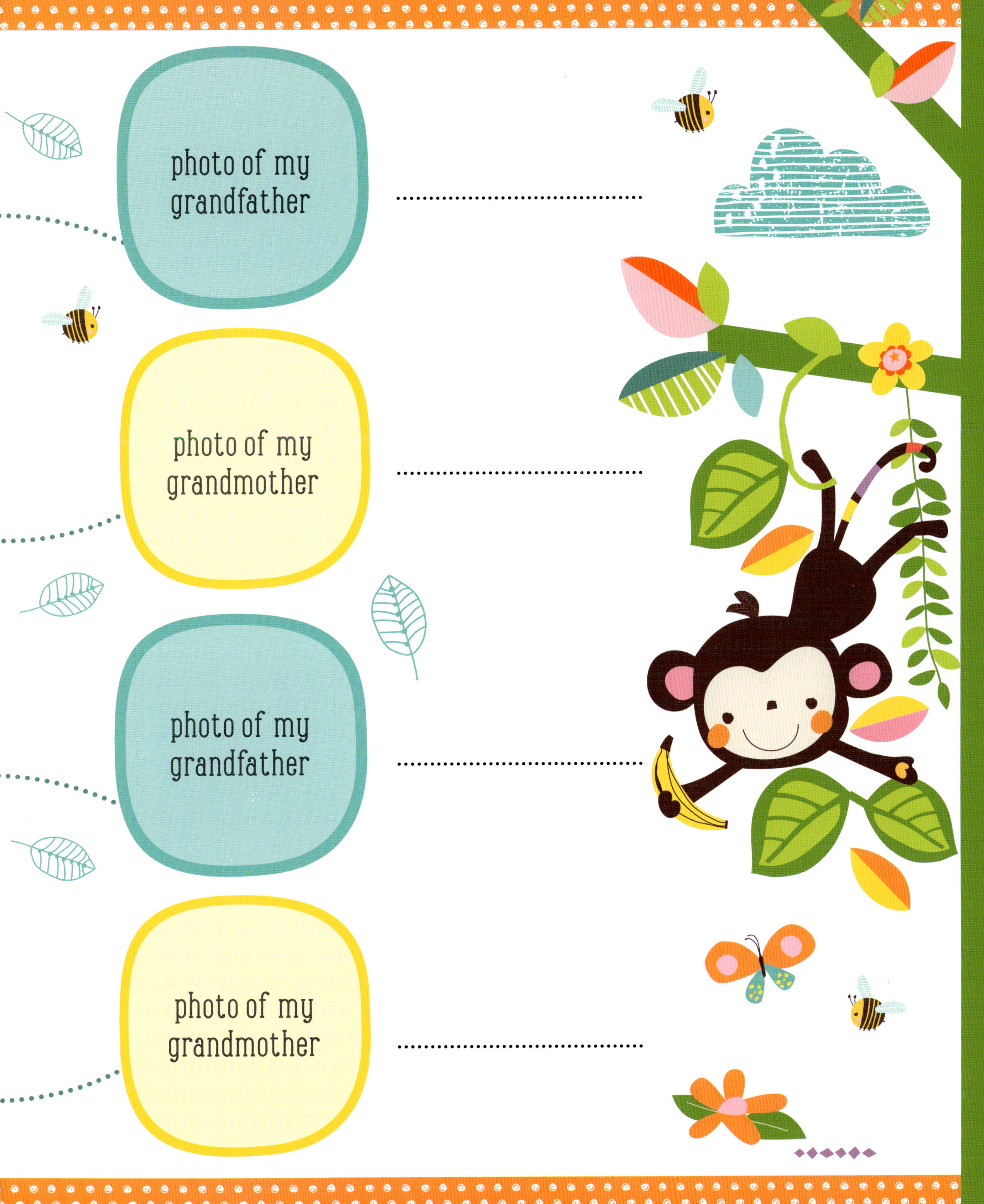
photo of my grandfather
photo of my grandmother
photo of my grandfather
photo of my grandmother

My Daddy

His birthday is

....

His eyes are

....

....

His hair is

....

photo

My Mommy

Her birthday is

....

Her eyes are

....

....

photo

Her hair is

....

All About Me

I was born on

....

....

I was born in this place:

....

....

The time was

....

My full name is ....

....

This name was chosen because

....

....

....

....

....

....

My weight was

....

My length was

....

My hair was

....

My eyes were

....

Where I Was Born

photo

The name of the place I was born was

....

....

The doctor and midwife were called

....

....

More about this special time:

....

....

....

These people came to visit me:
....
....
....
....
....
....
....
....
Here are some photos!
photo
photo
photo

The Day I Was Born

This was the number-one song:

....

....

....

....

This was the headline in the news:

....

....

....

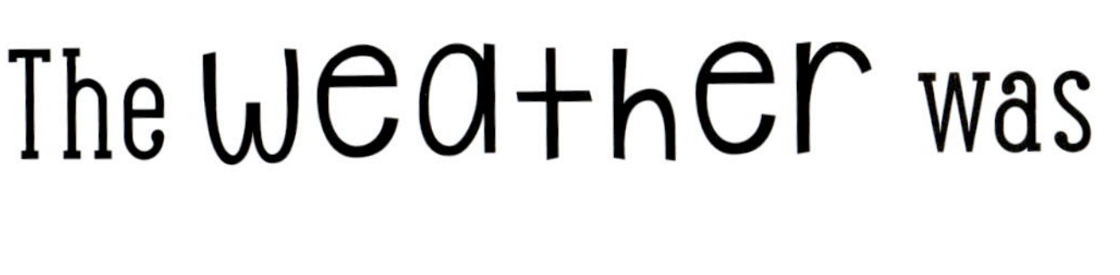

The weather was

....

I share my birthday with this famous person:

....

The president was

....

Coming Home

My first day at home was

....

I was

happy

grumpy

sleepy

wide awake

My first diaper was changed by

....

....

....

photo

Here's a print of my hand:

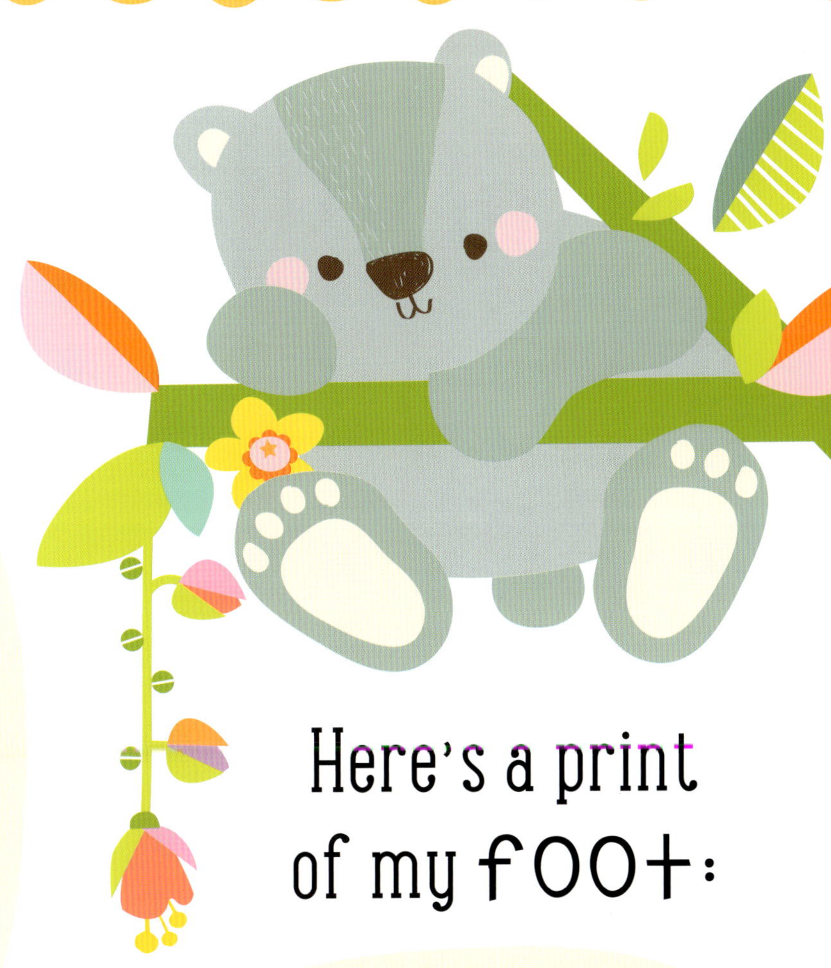

Here's a print of my foot:

Here's my hospital bracelet:

The VIPS in My Life

Here are some very important people in my life.

This is

....

He/She is my

....

This is

....

He/She is my

....

photo
This is
He/She is my
photo
This is
He/She is my

My Firsts

I slept
through the night
for the
first time
on

....

I slept in my
bassinet
for the
first time
on

....

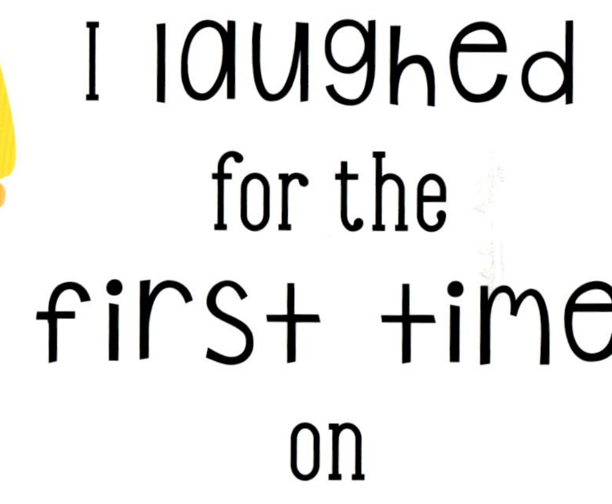

I laughed
for the
first time
on

....

I smiled
for the
first time
on

....

I got my
first tooth
on

....

I was

....

months old.

I ate
my first
solid meal
on

....

It was

....

....

....

....

My Firsts

I rolled over
for the
first time
on

....

photo

photo

I sat up
for the
first time
on

....

I crawled
for the
first time
on

....

photo
I stood up
for the
first time
on
....
photo
photo
I played my
first game
of peekaboo
on
....

My Firsts

I went **swimming** for the **first time** on

....

I **walked** with help for the **first time** on

....

I **waved** for the **first time** on

....

I waved to

....

More first moments for Mommy and Daddy to add!

My First Words
I said my first word on
....
It was
....
Here is what happened:
....
....
....
....

Here are the next four words I said and who I said them to:

My First Day Out

I went to

....

....

....

....

I went with these people:

....

....

....

....

....

....

....

....

Some Things to Remember

photo

photo

My First Party

photo

These people were there:

....

....

....

....

....

....

The party was for:

....

Some Things to Remember:

photo

photo

photo

A Few Of My Favorite Things!

photo

These are my favorite toys:

....

....

....

....

This is my favorite food:

....

....

....

This is my favorite thing to do:

....

....

....

This is my favorite place:

....

....

....

....

photo

I Am One Year Old!
1
photo
1
My weight is
....
My height is
....

My eyes are
....
People think I look like
....
....
My hair is
....
....
photo
I now have
....
teeth!

Here's a new print
of my foot:
Here's a new print
of my hand:
photo